Reptiles

Joy Richardson

W
FRANKLIN WATTS
LONDON • SYDNEY

This edition 2003
Franklin Watts
96 Leonard Street
London EC2A 4XD

Franklin Watts Australia
45-51 Huntley Street
Alexandria
NSW 2015

Editors: Sarah Ridley and Sally Luck
Designer: Janet Watson
Illustrator: Angela Owen
Picture Researcher: Sarah Moule

Photographs: Bruce Coleman Ltd 7tl, 7tr, 13, 15,
21; Frank Lane Picture Agency front cover, title
page, 16, 23, 27; Natural History Photographic
Agency 7br, 18, 24; Oxford Scientific Films/Animals
Animals 7bl, 8, 10

A CIP catalogue record for this book is available from the British Library
Dewey Decimal Classification 597.9

ISBN: 0 7496 5315 9

Printed in Malaysia

Contents

07488

Reptile relations

Snakes, lizards, crocodiles, alligators, tortoises and turtles all belong to a group of animals called reptiles.

Reptiles before people
Reptiles lived on earth at the same time as the **dinosaurs** - millions and millions of years ago.

Most reptiles today are quite small. All reptiles have bodies which work in the same sort of way.

▶ These animals are all reptiles.

Reptile babies

Reptiles have babies by laying eggs.

Laying eggs
Reptile mothers lay eggs. They hide them so
that other animals cannot find and eat them.
The eggs are soft and leathery.

Breaking out
Baby reptiles break out of their egg with
the help of an **egg tooth** on their **snout**.
This tooth drops off later.

Newborn reptiles
The **newborn** babies look like little adults.
They can move about and feed themselves
as soon as they are born. Most get no help
from their parents.

◄   These baby snakes are
breaking out of their eggs.

9

Growing bigger

Most reptiles **shed** their skin as they grow bigger.

Snake skins
Snakes have a top layer of skin which has no colour. As they grow, this layer comes loose from the brightly coloured skin below. Snakes then wriggle out of this old skin, leaving an empty tube behind.

Lizard skins
Lizard skins crack and flake off when they grow bigger.

◀ This snake is shedding its skin.

Tough skin

Reptiles have tough skin covered with hard **scales**, like fingernails.

Protection from the sun
Their tough skin helps to protect them from the sun. It stops them from drying out in the heat.

Protection from enemies
Most reptiles cannot move very fast. Their tough scaly skin helps to protect them from enemies.

Slow-moving tortoises have even more protection. They have a thick, bony **shell** on their back which they can hide inside if they are in danger.

▶ This crocodile's tough, scaly skin helps to protect it from enemies.

Camouflage

Many reptiles have skin which looks the same as their surroundings.
This is called **camouflage**.

Some lizards are camouflaged.
Speckled lizards hide easily on sandy rocks.
Patterned snakes slither through stones
and leaves without being seen.

Changing colours

Many reptiles change colour. Chameleons
change colour very quickly when
they want to creep up on insects or
when they want to hide.

▶ This chameleon
has turned
green to be
camouflaged
amongst the
green leaves.

Temperature control

All reptiles are **cold-blooded**. Their body **temperature** depends on the temperature outside.

Living in the sun
Reptiles cannot keep themselves warm so they live mainly in hot sunny places.

Reptiles are active only when their temperature feels right. In between they take longs rests. They lie in the sun to warm up and hide in the shade to cool down.

Hibernating
In winter, reptiles **hibernate** and do nothing until the weather warms them up again.

◄   This lizard is lying in the sun to warm up its body temperature.

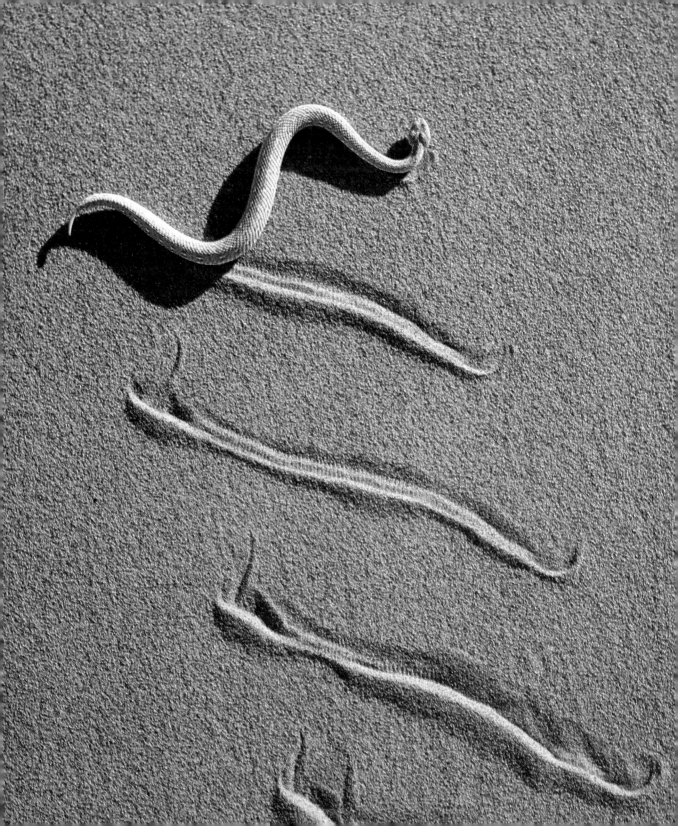

Skeletons

All reptiles have a skeleton inside. They have a backbone from head to tail and most have four legs.

Bending and wiggling

Snakes have no legs but they have hundreds of tiny bones in their backbone. This makes them very flexible. They can bend and wiggle and coil up.

Leaving their tails behind

Lizards scurry along with their legs sticking out on each side. They can break off their tail and leave it behind if they are attacked.

◄ A side-winder snake moves by bending its body to jump over the sand.

Snake skeleton

Reptiles are land creatures but some like the water.

Crocodiles and alligators

Crocodiles and alligators live in rivers and **swamps** and use their tails for swimming. They lay eggs on the land and crawl around on their stomach and stumpy legs.

Turtles

Turtles come out of the sea to lay their eggs in the sand. When they are born, baby turtles flap their way back to the sea as quickly as possible.

▶ These newborn turtles are making their way across the sand, into the sea.

Eating a meal

Reptiles have jaws which open really wide to catch food.

Eating large animals
Snakes have a stretchy mouth. This means they can catch animals which are larger than them and swallow them whole!

Some snakes **inject** victims with **poison** from their teeth. Some snakes curl round and squeeze them to death.

Small appetites
Snakes **digest** their food slowly. They can go for weeks between meals.

Reptiles use no energy keeping warm, so they do not need much to eat.

▶ This snake is swallowing a large frog whole.

Reptile senses

Reptiles see, hear and smell in a different way to people.

Seeing
Most reptiles have eyes which always stay open. Snakes' eyes are covered with **transparent** eyelids, so they never need to blink.

Hearing
Reptiles have sound openings on their head but no ear flaps.

Smelling and breathing
Snakes and lizards flick out long tongues to find smells in the air. They have nostrils to breathe air into their lungs.

◀   This reptile uses its tongue to smell.

Growing old

Most animals stop growing when they become adults but reptiles never stop growing.

Growth rings
A tortoise's **shell** grows bigger all the time, except when it is hibernating. A new **growth ring** forms on its shell each year. The number of rings tell us how old the tortoise is.

The giant tortoise
Some giant tortoises can live to be over a hundred years old.

▶ Growth rings form in each section of a tortoise's shell.

The tiniest lizard,
the longest snake,
the slowest tortoise
and the fiercest crocodile all
have some things in common.

All reptiles lay eggs. They keep growing
until the die. They have dry scaly skins.
They are cold-blooded.

Glossary

camouflage The patterns and colours on skin which help an animal hide by making it look like part of its surroundings.

cold-blooded Cold-blooded animals cannot keep their blood at the same temperature. It heats up and cools down with the outside temperature.

digest To break down food inside the body, after it has been eaten.

dinosaur A giant animal that lived on earth millions of years ago.

egg tooth A hard point which baby reptiles have on their snouts to help them break out of their shell.

growth ring The rings that grow on a tortoise's shell each year, showing how old it is.

hibernate To hide away and sleep during the cold winter.

inject To put liquid into the body by making a hole in the skin.

newborn Only just born.

poison A substance that can damage or kill living things.

scales Thin plates of hard skin that cover and protect a reptile's body.

shed When the top layer of a reptile's skin comes off.

shell A hard, protective case attached to some animal's bodies.

snout Area of the head including the mouth and nose.

swamp An area of land where the earth is very muddy and full of water.

temperature The temperature of something is how hot or cold it is.

transparent See-through.

Index